W9-AVI-930

The Book of Finnish Elves

Written and illustrated by
MAURI KUNNAS

Translated from the Finnish by
Tim Steffa

Otava Publishing Company Ltd Helsinki

ELVES

Back in the old days, when Grandma's great-grandfather's mother was still just a tiny little tot, many homes had guardian spirits. Their task was to fend off misfortune and bring good luck to the household. These guardian spirits were called elves.

Each sort of building had its own sort of elf. Houses had household elves, saunas had sauna elves, barns barn elves, stables stable elves, and mills mill elves.

In ages past there were actually all kinds of other curious beings as well, such as sprites, gnomes, goblins, brownies, fairies, imps, pixies, will-o'-the-wisps, wights and whatnot. Life was pretty exciting back then, wasn't it?

Elves had lived around people since way back when, long before Santa Claus was born.

Elves kept out of sight. They loved dark places and preferred to move about at nighttime or at dusk. So elves weren't often seen. As a rule they were heard instead, knocking somewhere in a dim corner or attic. "That wouldn't be an elf tapping, would it?" folks used to say.

3

All the same, it occasionally happened that as someone was entering their house they'd catch a glimpse of a red cap as an elf scurried behind the stove. But this occured so seldom that, for years after, people would pass the twilight hours retelling it.

Elves grew to an advanced age. They lived for hundreds of years, which is why they had such impressive whiskers. They were small in size, their men and womenfolk no taller than a five-year-old child.

They usually wore red stocking caps, grey jackets or black waistcoats, and big boots. But there was also variety to the elderly elves' attire. One might wear a felt cap, another a tall stovepipe hat, while a third might go about bare-headed. Some wore fur coats and some, knee britches. One household boasted a cocky, brass-buttoned officer elf. Sheepskin tunics were popular among their womenfolk, but blue dresses, white stockings and high-buttoned shoes were not altogether alien to the wardrobe of the female elf.

Some elves had only one eye. These were usually in the middle of their foreheads and as big as saucers. These elves generally lived in threshing barns, where they'd sit before the big drying kilns with clouds of smoke billowing from their long churchwarden pipes.

THE FIDDLER ELF

On one farm there lived a fiddler elf. He had a battered old violin that he liked to scrape on at night up in the dark of the attic. He usually played softly, so his fiddling was no cause for complaint, aside from the scampering of mice on the attic floor. They loved it when the elf played and the music made them dance all over the attic. Otherwise, the elf was no trouble. They were decent, hardworking folks on the place, and the elf wouldn't have dreamed of disturbing them.

One time hay-making chanced to fall during the full moon. Everyone had a hard day toiling under a blazing sun, and when evening came they all fell fast asleep. Except for the master of the household. He was a light sleeper and the full moon made him restless. Try as he might, he simply could not get to sleep.

He wasn't the only one in the house who was driven to distraction by that great big moon. The old fiddler elf sat at the little attic window, sawing at his fiddle and gazing at the moon with sad, wide eyes. He was recalling the long-lost good old days (as only a centuries-old elf can) and pondering the future. So deep was he under the moon's spell that he didn't notice he was playing louder and louder. It wasn't long before the lonely elf's scraping carried all the way to the restless master's ears. He tossed and turned in his bed and tried covering his head with a pillow. But nothing helped. The music just seemed to grow louder. Finally, he'd had enough. He flung himself out of bed, banged on the ceiling with his knobbly walking stick, and shouted: "Quiet up there, you infernal elf! You don't even know how to play! All you can do is saw at it!"

That was more than the elf could tolerate. "So I don't know how to play, eh?" he said, starting up a polka that sent the tables and chairs skittering around the downstairs floor. For the rest of the night there wasn't a single soul in the household who got so much as a wink of sleep. And out in the hayfield next morning, the yawns were so big and wide that they even put the full moon to shame.

FEETU-OF-THE-GARRET

Elves had peculiar names – for example, Fetlock, Noggin, Scalawag, Slapdash, Whirliwight, Hobgobble and Tinsel.

On one farm there was an elf called Feetu-of-the-Garret. He'd acquired that name because he lived in the attic of the house – which was also called the garret – where he'd collected a big heap of old rugs at the foot of the chimney. It was warm there whenever the oven was heated downstairs. That made it just the place for an old elf to loll. What is more, the household took good care of Feetu. Each week a big steaming bowl of porridge was set out for him at the foot of the attic stairs. Feetu was one contented elf.

It came time once more to do the household baking. The mistress of the house was in the habit of always giving Feetu, who was known to be a hearty eater, the first loaf of the batch. That was her way of making sure the household never ran short of bread. You see, if elves were kept in good spirits, they brought good harvests to the farms. As long as there was enough grain, there was enough bread.

The fragrance of freshly baked bread soon filled the house and drifted up through the attic door to Feetu's big nose. The old fellow's mouth commenced to water.

But, oh, what an unlucky day that was! A new and somewhat devious servant by the name of Alma had just entered the household, and it was to her that the mistress entrusted a basket holding the first oven-fresh loaf to take to the attic stairs. Alma didn't believe in anything she hadn't seen with her own two eyes, and

to her it was downright foolish to leave such wonderful bread on the stairs where mice could nibble at it. So as soon as she was out in the vestibule where she knew the mistress couldn't see her, she gobbled down the whole loaf. Then she went back inside.

Feetu-of-the-Garret waited until he was certain no one was around and then peeped cautiously from the attic doorway. The basket was empty. Not a single crumb of bread. Feetu felt not only surprised, but somewhat betrayed as well. He just couldn't believe that the mistress would ever play such a nasty trick on him. Maybe she'd scorched the first loaves. Of course. That had to be it.

Feetu returned to the foot of the chimney to wait.

Time passed and the baking continued downstairs. After a while the elf went over to the doorway again, but the basket was just as empty as ever. Then Feetu-of-the-Garret – who was ordinarily a very peaceable elf – completely lost his temper. He began to kick up such a ruckus in the attic that it threatened to raze the roof. So powerful was he that he even sent a big wooden tub crashing down through the ceiling, knocking a table over. The mistress and maid fled the house in a flurry of flour.

When Feetu saw that everyone was gone, he crept down and found a huge heap of freshly baked bread. That put a sudden halt to his crankiness. The elf gobbled up every single delicious loaf. And as he clambered back up to the attic with a stomach ache, he decided that there wasn't all that much to get upset about. You never really know what to expect with people. So he forgot the whole thing.

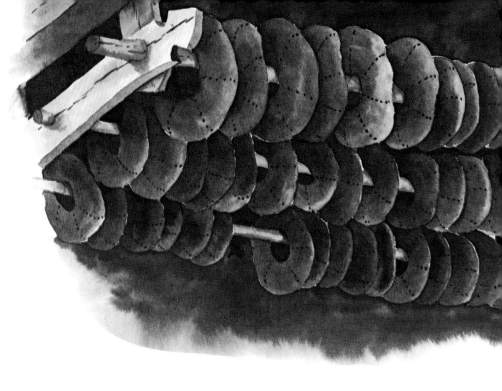

Feetu's fit had thrown such a scare into Alma that she left the household for good. The mistress and master, for their part, feared that in his rage Feetu would abandon them and take their harvest luck with him.

But there was no cause for concern. Feetu-of-the-Garret wouldn't have traded anything for his snug rugs in the attic. Otherwise, he would no longer have been Feetu-of-the-Garret.

The only unfortunate consequence for the household was that they couldn't find a new maid anywhere... if you can call that unfortunate.

FETLOCK
THE HOUSEHOLD ELF

The preferred abode of household elves were the dark sleeping lofts over ovens. There they could idle away the days out of human sight.

Over the oven in one house there lived an elf by the name of Fetlock. He wasn't quite your ordinary household elf in that one of his feet resembled a horse's hoof. This peculiarity had gained him a good deal of fame. People came from all over to wonder at his handsome hoof. This elf wasn't particularly shy about human company. On the contrary, he'd gladly flash his horse's hoof from the oven loft for folks to marvel at.

But Fetlock had another characteristic for which he was also famous. To absolutely no man would he ever yield his place over the oven. Intruders were expelled without mercy. Many a strong man had given it a try, but all had come tumbling to the floor.

Once a really stubborn traveller happened to stop at the house. He asked the folks on the place if he might possibly spend the night in the oven loft.

"You'd best ask the elf," he was told.

The traveller didn't believe much in elves, so he said with a sneer: "This is one man who has yet to beg leave of any elf." And up the few steps to the loft he climbed.

He was just dropping off to sleep when he was sent crashing to the floor.

The hired hands bunked down in the room began to chuckle. "Now will you believe you can't sleep there?" they asked the traveller.

"I'll sleep where I like," the man growled, "and I don't intend to fall to the floor again. Of that you can be sure." And back up to the loft he clambered.

After a short while a tremendous crash sounded near the oven, but there was no sign of the traveller tumbling to the floor. The hired hands were astonished. Had Fetlock finally met his match?

But as dawn broke and folks started out on their morning chores, they found the travelling bully out behind the house, fast asleep in a ditch. That was how far the elf had pitched him. And as a reminder the elf had also planted a hoofprint on his backside.

So the man was right when he said he hadn't intended to fall to the floor again...

THE LITTLE OLD BIDDY ELF

Household elves relished cleanliness and order. They thrived in homes where, before bedtime, floors were swept clean and dishes were washed and stacked neatly on shelves. Chairs, benches, bins and other large objects had to be put back in place so that they weren't in the elves' way during their nightly tours of inspection.

In diligent households where spinning, planing and whittling went on until late at night, sleep sometimes caught folks by surprise, and floors didn't get swept. So at night the elves would sweep the leavings into neat little piles in the corners of rooms. That was their way of helping hardworking folks. But such elves were rare.

In one house there was a tiny grey female elf who was renowned for her cantankerous nature. She demanded complete cleanliness and order from the folks on the place and would tolerate no laziness, let along any other naughty behavior. Though the mistress of the household was anything but lazy, she was often in trouble with this elfin fussbudget.

When night came the old biddy elf would clamber down from her place over the oven and begin her regular inspection of the household. If the floor wasn't swept to her standards, she'd stomp around until the house shook: "GET UP, WOMAN! SWEEP THIS FLOOR AND GIVE ME ROOM TO MOVE!" All the mistress could do was crawl meekly out of bed and take up her broom. If the elf wasn't obeyed, she's raise such a ruckus that sleep was out of the question for the entire household.

The mistress once left a few unwashed dishes on the table by accident. The old biddy elf flew into a rage. She yanked the broom from its corner, scrambled up on the table – and that's when the rumpus started. Cups, bowls, candlesticks, buckets – the elf hurled them all into a corner of the room. The household woke with a start. Convinced a gang of thieves was storming the place, the master of the house wound up scuffling with the elf. Such was the fray that they even sent big wooden tubs reeling.

Eventually the tiny but obstinate elf calmed down and retreated to the darkness of the loft above the oven. But it wasn't until well into the next day that they got that room straightened up again.

SAMI SOOTSNOUT THE SAUNA ELF

Sauna elves were easy to identify because they were entirely sooty and black. Back in the olden days saunas had no chimneys, so when they were heated all the smoke stayed inside. It's little wonder that any elf who dwelt in a dark, sooty sauna loft eventually turned completely black.

In the loft of a sauna on one farm there lived an elf by the name of Sami Sootsnout. He'd lived there for a couple of centuries, so he was really and truly black, right to the very tip of his nose – which is how he got his name. Sootiness didn't bother elves. On the contrary, it was well nigh a source of pride. It was this that set sauna elves apart.

One Easter the sauna had been heated up and the folks on the place were just finishing their bath. They made it a practise when leaving the sauna to fill it with a final head of steam because they knew how the elf loved to loll in the hot loft. The only difference this time was that the woman of the house took it into her head to fill a tub with hot water so for once the elf would have a chance to bathe.

There the big wooden tub of water stood, awaiting Sami. "I'll give it a try," thought old Sootsnout, and down from the loft he scrambled. He sniffed the water and tested it cautiously with his finger. Something about it made him uneasy, but in the end his curiosity got the best of him. He removed his sooty shirt, trousers and boots. Splashing water from the brimming tub, the elf settled in to his bath. "Not half bad, this bathing business," he chuckled to himself as he watched his sooty beard float on the warm water.

It felt so good that the old fellow dozed off and didn't wake up until dawn. With a start, he leaped out of the water. Good grief! It had washed away his wonderful soot! Sami Sootsnout, right down to the every last whisker of his beard, had gone completely pale.

This was too much for the sauna elf. "Old Sami's not a sootsnout any more," he groaned as he pulled on his black trousers. Miserable as he was, he happened to glance at the water in the tub, where he saw his own reflection.

Lo and behold, his big nose wasn't white! It was just as pitch-black as ever. Sami hadn't, of course, put his nose in the water, so it had remained sooty. What a huge relief this was to the old elf. No matter how clean the rest of him was, he was still the same old Sami Sootsnout.

In time, of course, the rest of him became just as sooty as before. So no damage had been done.

But after that, whenever the mistress filled a bath for Sami, next morning the tub was always found bottom-up in a corner somewhere – which goes to show just how much Sami's black nose had been put out of joint.

THE BATTLE OF
THE HARVEST ELVES

Not only did elves bring farmfolk luck, they were also known to return from their nocturnal wanderings with genuine loot. Such elves were called harvest or grain elves. They brought grist and seed to granaries, added to woodpiles, and sometimes even left real money in their masters' pockets. However, an elf's contributions to domestic coffers were, more often than not, at a neighbor's expense.

In one area a homestead called the Mikkola farm boasted an exceptionally eager harvest elf. In another village nearby, on the Kela farm, there was another diligent elf. Both spent their nights hard at work, each doing his best to see to it that his homeplace prospered. Now, the Mikkola place had no mill, but it did have a sizeable forest; and while there were no woods to speak of on the Kela farm, there was a good mill. So flour was what the Mikkola elf generally fetched home, and the Kela elf brought firewood. And that meant they each visited the other's place fairly often.

Once, as both elves were returning home from foraging trips, they happened to meet between the two farms on a bridge. The Mikkola elf had three whole barrels' worth of Kela flour hidden up his big sleeves, and the Kela elf had a cord or more of Mikkola firewood concealed beneath his shirt. They faced off on the bridge, each wondering just what the other was up to.

"You took something, didn't you?" one asked.

"I did if you did," the other answered back. And before long a scuffle broke out on the bridge. Each elf seized the other's shirtfront, pushing and pulling with all his might. The Kela elf tried to snatch the flour from the Mikkola elf, and the other way around.

The ensuing fracas on the bridge woke up folks in all directions. They assumed a thunderstorm was raging. Neither elf could best the other. Finally the one from Kela managed to tear open his adversary's shirt sleeve, and out spilled the flour. But he was unlucky enough to get so much of it in his eyes that he couldn't see a thing, and it was then that the Mikkola elf tore open his shirt. The firewood fell in a heap at the Mikkola elf's feet, and he tripped over it and fell head-first into the river.

The Kela elf was so blinded by flour that when he set out for home he ran in the wrong direction. And the current carried the Mikkola elf several miles downstream before he managed to drag himself ashore. It was late morning before the two crestfallen elves finally got home.

After that the Kela elf stayed away from the Mikkola farm and the Mikkola elf stayed away from the Kela farm. They chose instead to live in mutual and everlasting harmony and respect.

THE HARVEST ELF
AND THE BUTTONS

On one farm there was a very old barn. It was so old that the folks on the place decided to build a new one and use the old barn to store wagons and sledges and other agricultural implements. But as the years passed it become so dilapidated that one winter, after unusually heavy snows, its roof caved in and the whole thing collapsed in a heap.

"Oh, cinders and flinders!" said Pekka, the head of the household. Pekka was renowned for the power of his oaths. "So it finally fell down. It's a good thing there was no one inside."

"No people," his old grandpappy muttered, "but what about the elf?" You see, Grandpappy could remember how, when he was still a little boy, the old folks used to tell about the barn's guardian spirit, otherwise known as a harvest elf. But that had been so long ago that Grandpappy was now an old man.

That spring, after most of the snow had melted, Pekka was hauling a load of timber from the forest. As he and his horse were passing the ruins of the barn, he suddenly heard a soft lament coming from among the logs.

"By the billy goat's beard," Pekka exclaimed, "who can that be?"

"I have no roof over my head...," a voice mourned.

Pekka had no idea it was the elf. He figured some poor soul had lost his way, so he shouted: "Climb aboard and I'll take you to our place!" No sooner had

spoken than the sledge gave such a lurch that it nearly dumped him on the ground. It felt exactly as if someone had jumped on behind, but Pekka didn't see a soul.

"Oh, shirt sleeves! There's something funny here," thought Pekka. The sledge had become so heavy that the horse could barely haul it home. Stranger still, as they passed the sauna it gave another lurch and the sauna door slammed. This lightened the load again and left Pekka wondering: "Oh, jam jars and jellybeans! I hope that wasn't the elf!"

But it was the elf, the very same elf old Grandpappy had mentioned. He'd probably gone to sleep back when Grandpappy was still just a little tyke, and the barn coming down around his ears had awakened him. He'd been sitting there all alone, grieving the loss of house and home, when Pekka came along and gave him a ride.

You see, without a home to call his own, the elf wasn't really an elf. But now, in Pekka's sauna, contentment was his once more.

Pretty soon strange things began to happen around the farm. The old guardian spirit – harvest elf that he was – began to bring all manner of things to the place. Grain appeared in the granary and wood on the woodpile. Naturally, Pekka was not only perplexed but pleased as well.

One time, as Pekka stepped out to the stable to see to the horses, he bumped into the elf – a little old codger with an empty sack over his shoulder.

"What'll it be this time?" he asked Pekka in his gravely voice.

Pekka, who'd never actually seen this infernal harvest elf, was sorely amazed. "Oh, bushels of vest buttons!" he hollered, hightailing it home to hide beneath his bed.

When the rooster crowed next morning, Pekka crawled out of hiding and... good heavens! Heaped in bowls, buckets and baskets, piled on the floor, benches, tables and shelves were so many shiny vest buttons that Pekka could barely wade through them!

The elf went on bringing vest buttons to Pekka's house for nine nights, until there must have been bushels of them. Even for the old harvest elf this was such an enormous undertaking that afterwards he went straight to sleep in the dark sauna and probably didn't wake up again until it was the sauna's turn to collapse about his ears.

The only thing Pekka could do was sell the buttons at the marketplace in town. He did get quite a fair sum for them, at any rate. But it must have cost him a good many billy goat's beards and other oaths before he'd rid himself of them.

THE BARN ELF'S
NEW CLOTHES

On some farms elves tended the livestock. It might be that a place had a barn elf – generally a little old lady – or a bustling stable elf in the form of a little old gent.

On one farm the guardian of the barn was one of these little old ladies. She'd lived in the loft for ages. She faithfully fed and curried the cows, cleaned their stalls, brought them hay to eat, and chatted with them on long winter nights. Such a little helper was a blessing to the mistress of the household. A tidy barn made morning milking a pleasure.

Once, as the mistress was entering the barn, she saw the elf. She caught a glimpse of a patched skirt as the elf ducked out of sight in a manger.

"A patched skirt...," she thought. "I'll wager the poor thing has but that one tattered and mended dress..."

She was beginning to feel rather sorry for the guardian spirit when a thought suddenly struck her: "I'll have new clothes made for you as a reward for all the trouble you've gone to. It's the least I can do."

Not long after that an itinerant tailor came by to sew new clothes for the folks on the place. He made new aprons and skirts for the servant girl and new trousers for the hired hands. The mistress also ordered a new garment for her little helper. But for some reason she suddenly took a notion to order a party frock for the elf instead of a decent work skirt.

"In this household not even the small fry go around in patches," she boasted huffishly to the tailor. "They're to dress up."

As soon as the dress was ready the mistress took it to the barn and spread it on an overturned tub where the elf was sure to find it.

Night came and the guardian spirit came down from her loft. "What in the world is that black rag doing draped on the tub? Why, it looks to me like a dress," she said in amazement. Well, it was a dress, and a fine one at that.

She carefully felt it. What excellent cloth it was made of – soft and fine. Nothing like her own coarse work skirt. Ever so gently she picked it up for a closer look.

"Why, goodness me, it's just my size!"

The delighted elf broke into a smile. In a wink she'd scampered up to the loft and tossed her tattered old clothes into a corner. The darned old ancient rags. With

trembling hands she put on her new black party frock. Would she ever be the same old barn elf again?

Down from the loft she proudly climbed to show off her new togs to the surprised cows. "Moo, moo, do you look fine! But what about our hay?" the cows inquired.

"Hay? Why, that would soil my new gown," snapped the elf. "No, sirree, not tonight..." And around the barn she strutted with her nose in the air, like some sort of princess.

When the mistress came to do the morning milking, she found that the barn hadn't been cleaned at all. She didn't know what to think. What had gotten in to her little helper? She'd never neglected her duties before. And when the same thing happened the next morning, and the one after that, the mistress began to get good and worried. With so much for her to do around the house, she couldn't possibly manage to keep the barn as neat as the elf had. And so, as the days passed, the barn became more and more untidy.

A week went by with the elf strutting, prancing and flirting about the barn. You could tell from the cows that she'd so completely forgotten about her work that she no longer seemed to know which end of a broom was up.

But one night, as she was flirting again with the cattle, she accidentally stepped in a milk pail the mistress had left in the middle of the floor. KER-PLUNK! The elf flopped to the dirty floor. "What lazybones left everything topsy-turvy?" she grumbled. "And just look at the rest of this place!"

She got to her feet in a huff and grabbed her broom. Dust swirled and dirt flew as the old biddy fussed and bustled around the barn.

The cows chuckled. "If it isn't our old aunty elf," they lowed.

But the old biddy was so busy cleaning that she didn't hear a thing. She swept every last nook and cranny, and washed and curried the cows from their horns to the tips of their tails. Dawn found her leaning on her broom and panting.

In the heat of her cleaning fit, she'd forgotten about her fine apparel. Her gown was covered with dirt. She looked at herself gloomily. As the cows mooed at the top of their voices, the elf was suddenly struck by the humor of her predicament. "Who cares about clothes?" she said. The world had all the snobs it needed, but good barn elves were few and far between.

The next morning the mistress was overjoyed to find the barn neat and clean. Except for a scrap of black cloth in the middle of the floor, everything was in its place. She understood at once. The elf had returned to work.

The mistress never again made the mistake of providing the elf with new clothes.

THE STABLE ELF
AND THE PEAS

A certain farm once boasted a particularly diligent stable elf. He'd taken on the task of tending the horses all by himself. There were two of them on the place, and their good health and fine form were admired by the entire village. All the master had to do each

evening was lead them through the stable door, and when he went to fetch them in the morning, the elf had fed them and curried them until they shined. He'd bring them hay from the stable mow, water them, mix mash for them in a big trough, keep their stalls clean, and even neatly braid their tails. Because this happened regularly every night, the head of the household never had to bother about tending them himself. That elf was the master's pride and joy.

No one had ever actually seen the elf. He was always up and about at night and did his chores so quietly that he never disturbed any of the folks on the place.

The lady of the house was very inquisitive. She was fascinated by this stable guardian and always asking the menfolk what sort of shapes these elves assumed. No one could give her a satisfactory answer though, because no one had ever seen him. The woman's curiosity just kept on growing until finally it got so she could think of little else. Always one and the same question: what did the stable elf look like?

In the end she could no longer contain herself, so she asked her husband if he'd mind her hiding some night in the stable. Afraid she'd upset the elf, he forbid it. But she whimpered and whined until her husband finally gave in, on condition that she wasn't to disturb the elf in any way.

When evening arrived the mistress crept to the stable. From her hiding place in a haystack she could snoop in secret on the old elf's activities.

Night came and hours went by. The woman peered from the haystack and listened. The horses stirred in

their stalls and mice scampered across the stable floor, but she couldn't make out any elfin sounds. What was more, the stable was pitch-dark. She couldn't see beyond the tip of her nose. She became discouraged. Even if she did hear the elf's footsteps, she wouldn't be able to see a thing.

She didn't hear a single unusual sound all night.

The coming of dawn didn't improve matters for this inquisitive woman. Just the opposite. She became grumpier than ever when she found that the horses' tails had been braided during the night. Somehow that darned elf had managed to do his chores without her noticing. The scalawag moved around altogether too silently!

The cranky mistress decided she'd do whatever it took to see the elf, and the following evening she coaxed her soft-hearted husband into letting her spend another night in the stable. This time she decided, despite her husband's warning, to set a trap for the elf.

She scattered dried peas all over the stable floor and the stairs to the mow so that anyone setting foot in the place would be in for a nasty spill. After that she hid in the haystack and waited. This time she'd also brought a candle along to light the instant she heard a sound. Darkness spread through the stable and mice began scratching in corners.

The hours dragged by. The mistress waited and waited. All of a sudden a loud commotion erupted on the stairs. With trembling fingers the woman lit the candle. And there he was – a flustered looking little duffer in a flurry of straw.

A glimpse of him was all she got. "IF I CAN'T DO MY WORK IN PEACE," he wheezed, "THEN I WON'T DO IT AT ALL!" And up the stairs and into the darkness of the mow he sprang.

The woman's satisfaction was short-lived. Next morning her husband found the stable empty. Both horses had disappeared, along with the elf. That was the price the household had to pay for the mistress' curiosity.

All the master could do was get new horses for the place. But on that farm beautifully braided horses' tails were forever a thing of the past.

THE BARN ELF

In the past one of the most important buildings on any farm was the threshing barn. They were big, dark and spooky buildings, but they suited elves just fine.

What were these barns used for? Toward the end of summer, when the grain had been reaped, it was bound into sheaves and carried by horses to the threshing barn. The sheaves were stowed there in spacious lofts. Then the barn's big drying kiln was heated up. It was kept heated day and night until the grain was properly dry. After that the grain was all ready for threshing.

It was during the heating of the barns that elves were often seen. Their job was to tend the fire in the kiln and to make sure that it didn't go out or that the kiln didn't overheat and set fire to the tinder-dry straw.

There was this one farm where the master was called Matti. He had a real gift for stoking kilns, so the barn-warming season kept him pretty busy. You see, once the fire had burned down, more wood had to be added, even if it was the middle of the night. Usually Matti's wife saw to it that he'd wake up to go to the barn before the fire in the kiln had burned out.

But once during grain-drying, she had to go and see her brother in a neighboring village. That put Matti in quite a fix. Since he slept like a log, how was he going to tend the kiln without his wife's help?

There was nothing Matti could do but try to stay awake all night. So when evening came he sat himself down before the hearth and watched as the glow of the fire played on the smudged log walls. Moisture from the sheaves of grain dripped monotonously to the floor, making Matti's eyelids droop.

Then he had a bright idea. He decided to stuff the kiln with as much firewood as it would hold. It was certain to last through the night and leave coals smoldering on the hearth until well into the morning. That way he wouldn't have to get up that night at all. Pleased with his plan, he filled the stove with wood and marched back to the house to sleep. He stretched

out on a bench, gladly forgot about the barn entirely, and fell fast asleep.

But during the night a strange thing happened. Matti's sweet slumbers were disturbed by someone grasping his big toe and trying to shake him awake. In his dreams Matti heard a whispering in his ear: "Matti, Matti, better see to your barn." And again: "Matti, Matti, better see to your barn."

But Matti wasn't so easily roused. Finally his toe was given such a firm jerk that he tumbled off the bench and crashed to the floor. That was enough to wake up even such a sound sleeper as Matti. He looked around at the dark room but couldn't see anyone.

"Better see to the barn?" he wondered. Why should he do that? But now that he was awake, he might just as well go and have a look. It couldn't do any harm.

Out into the darkness he went. He opened the barn door and... what on earth! A little old codger was scurrying to and fro before the kiln. With his cheeks all aglow, he was taking flaming logs from the stove with his bare hands. Matti figured some busybody from the village had come to the barn and he asked him: "Wha... what are you doing here?"

"You hush up!" the old fellow snapped. "You'd have burned down your barn if I hadn't kept watch." And in a single bound and a blur of whiskers, he disappeared behind the kiln.

It was then that Matti realized he'd been visited by an elf. The kiln was so hot that its stones glowed red. Filling it so full of firewood had been a fairly silly thing to do. And now he realized that the barn might very

well have burned down if the old elf hadn't stood guard. It was the elf who'd come to tweak Matti's toe and get him up.

"You looked after my barn, dear old elf," Matti said gratefully, "and I'll do the same for you."

And so grateful was he that from then on he gave the barn elf a big bowl of porridge every week. What is more, Matti never had to worry again about waking up, because when he went to bed he always left his big toe uncovered.

THE WRESTLER ELF
AND THE BEAR

Barn elves weren't always kind to visitors. If often happened that a weary traveller who'd stopped by a barn for the night had to leave before the evening was out because an elf was stomping around so hard in the loft that the wayfarer feared it would come crashing down around his ears. If a traveller wished to spend the night in a barn, the custom was to call out a greeting from the doorway and ask the guardian spirit for a night's lodging. If the elf didn't mind, a knocking sounded from a corner or the loft. If no sound was heard, the traveller knew that he might just as well continue on his way. There was no point in trying to sleep there; the elf would see to that one way or another.

Elves wouldn't stand for any sort of improper behavior in their barns. Drunkards and gamblers were evicted on the spot. Sometimes an elf would leap up on the drying kiln and shower such intruders with stones.

One farm had a barn in which there lived an elf who was a considerable burden to the folks on the place. The reason was that the elf was obsessed with wrestling. It wasn't that he was at all surly or cantankerous. Something simply moved him to challenge all comers to a test of wrestling skill. Since the villagers were familiar with the elf's ways, they avoided the barn; but many a weary traveller had stopped to rest there, only to end up getting a sample of the elf's hospitality. The minute he saw that a visitor

had dropped his bundle and dug out his provisions, the little red-capped fellow would peer down from the loft and demand: "Let's wrestle. Come on, let's wrestle." Generally the dumbfounded traveller couldn't even get a word out before he found himself hand-to-hand with the little gaffer.

Since the elf possessed the strength of several men, travellers didn't stand a chance of bettering him. Before long, the visitor would be flat on his back outside the barndoor, where the elf always threw his opponent at the finish of a match.

Once the oddest visitors came to the farm. A man arrived with a tame bear in tow and requested a night's lodging for himself and his beast. He travelled from village to village and town to town showing his unusual companion at marketplaces and fairs. The bear could do all sort of things, but dancing was its best trick – and also its favorite.

"The man's welcome to sleep in the house," came the answer to the request, "but we'll have to find somewhere else for the bear." The traveller had noticed the threshing barn beside the road and he suggested that the bear be put up there. At first the master of the place was reluctant, but then he figured that the elf probably wouldn't want to tangle with a bear. So since there really wasn't any other place available, the bear was shut up in the barn.

It was well into evening and the elf was roasting some mutton in the barn stove when the bear was thrust in the dark building. The elf sprang eagerly to his feet.

"Only travellers come to the barn at this hour," he

exclaimed, "and that means some wrestling fun." He was just about to invite the visitor to wrestle when he saw that it was actually an animal. "A dog," the elf snorted in disdain. He'd never in his life seen a bear before. So he went on roasting his mutton.

Its delicious fragrance wafted to the bear's wet nose. On the fair circuit the bear had mastered the art of begging for treats, so now it stood up on its hind feet and began to spin and dance daintily before the astonished elf.

The elf gazed in amazement. "You're no dog," he mumbled uncertainly. "To my knowledge, only people walk on two legs." Dancing made the bear look so human that the bewildered elf challenged it to a wrestling match. "Let's wrestle. Come on, let's wrestle," he squealed in excitement, grabbing hold of the bear. He grappled with all his might but that bear was as strong as... a bear. The more the elf grappled and grunted, the greater grew the bear's desire to dance. It reckoned it had found a real dancing partner in this little fellow and very tenderly embraced the elf in a bear hug.

No matter how the elf wriggled and squirmed, he couldn't get loose – let alone win. There was quite a rumpus in that barn as those two took each other's measure, one dancing and the other wrestling.

This went on for hours, until the elf was so exhausted that he couldn't even lift a finger. Eventually the bear let go of him. Weary and shamed, the elf crawled off to the darkness of the loft. In the meantime, the bear gobbled down the elf's roast. It had put on a fine and lengthy dancing display.

Defeat at the hands of the "hairy man" had dealt a severe blow to the elf's self-esteem. He took it so hard that he never again challenged anyone to wrestle. Of course, this was a welcome change for the villagers and the folks on the farm.

But to keep the elf from finding out what had really happened, no one mentioned the bout with the bear within earshot of the elf. If he had discovered that he'd actually tangled with a bear – who knows, it might have revived his interest in wrestling.

RAZE THE BARN

Back in the olden days, a good elf used to live on a place called the Reku farm. The folks there made sure that every Saturday a big bowl of porridge was set out for this elf. In return, he saw to it that they had good luck with their crops.

The years passed and the generations came and went. Eventually there was no one left to remember the elf but old Granny. Every Saturday she'd faithfully fill a bowl with porridge and take it someplace. No one ever bothered to find out where.

The young master of the house didn't believe at all in the elf. He made fun of the old lady and laughed as she bustled about. But that didn't bother her. "If you don't remember the elf," she said, "you'll bring misfortune on the household."

Before long Granny's weekly porridge deliveries began to annoy him. He had his own notions about the fate of that porridge. He was sure that some poor neighbor was taking advantage of Granny and eating it. Now, a dab of porridge wasn't about to ruin a rich household, but the young master was a man of principle: you don't give without getting something in return.

So one day he decided he'd put a stop to the old woman's foolishness. He spied on her as she filled the porridge bowl and took it out to "the elf." He stole along silently after her. The old woman carefully set the bowl on a flat rock behind the barn and returned home. The young master then played a mean trick. He hurried over to the bowl, dumped the perfectly good porridge on the ground, and filled the bowl with dirty ditchwater instead. Then he hid behind a corner of the barn. From there he'd have a clear view of his neighbor's expression when he stopped by for his weekly helping of porridge. The master was certain it was a neighbor who'd show up.

It wasn't very long either before the guest did appear. But what a peculiar looking neighbor! A tiny little old gent, all grey and bearded.

The master began to get a strange feeling in the pit of his stomach, but it was too late. The little fellow had already picked up the porridge bowl. And was he throwing a fit! Someone had ruined his porridge! He tossed the spoon furiously into the air and shouted: "RUIN THE PORRIDGE, RAZE THE BARN!" And before the master could recover from his shock, the strange apparition had run off.

The young master ended up paying dearly for his meanness. The next night the barn burned to the ground. The elf had taken his revenge.

Having to build a new barn made the young master amend his principles and change his ways. Each week he himself put a bowl of porridge behind the barn, and it wasn't but a couple years before the elf began once more to accept the offering.

THE MILL ELF

Mill elves were as white as sauna elves were sooty and black. Mills were where grain was ground into flour, and guardian spirits who lived their entire lives surrounded by flour were bound to turn pale.

One farm had a young hired hand by the name of Tuomas. Once, on Good Friday, his master ordered him to spend the night grinding grain at the mill. The mistress didn't like the idea one bit. Working in the mill on Good Friday – why, it was downright sacrilegious. "That may be," said the stern master, "but in this house my word is law." So Tuomas had to go.

Darkness was falling when Tuomas arrived at the mill. He let the water through the gate and dumped grain down the hopper. With a growl, the millstone began turning; and Tuomas looked to see that the grain was flowing into the eye of the mill.

The hours crept by. "What a way to spend the holiday," the boy thought gloomily. But so it goes. The mill groaned and Tuomas dozed.

Suddenly, at around midnight, a strange thing happened: the milled stopped dead. Tuomas awakened with a start. Something had gone wrong. When he opened the hatch to the wheelroom, he was so flabbergasted he nearly fell over. A tiny little old geezer was holding the millwheel tight in both hands.

"Wha... who are you?" the boy stammered. "What are you doing here? If you don't go away and let me get on with the milling, the master will be angry."

But old grizzly-grist just kept right on holding the wheel in his firm grip without saying a word.

Thomas' courage failed him and he couldn't think of anything better to do than make a beeline for the house. The master was grumpy at having his sleep disturbed. He didn't believe the boy one bit.

"You're just trying to get out of spending the night at the mill," he grumbled as he pulled on his trousers. "There's no man strong enough to stop that millwheel from turning."

But he went to the mill anyway, to see for himself; and sure enough, the mill had stopped. He stormed into the wheelroom and, goodness gracious, there was the little old man, his body braced, holding the millwheel still with his bare hands. The master couldn't believe his eyes. Who was this strongman? Well, whoever he was, he had no business interfering in the affairs of the household.

"You let go this instant!" bellowed the master. "I'm the master of this house and my word is law!"

"You may be the master of the house," snapped the little old man, "but I'm the master of this mill and I want to rest on my holiday. This is no time to make your boy do the milling." And with that, he disappeared right before the master's eyes.

That threw a scare into the master. Could that have been the mill's guardian spirit? To come face to face with an angry elf was no joking matter, that much the master knew. Frightened and cowed, he returned to the house. Tuomas didn't go back to the mill that night, or any other night. From then on all the farm's milling was done during the day so as never again to disturb the old elf's sleep.

THE ELF'S CHRISTMAS

Elves were taking part in Yuletide festivities long before there was a Santa Claus. Christmas, of course, was a celebration of Christ's birth, but it was also a harvest festival and no time for households to neglect their benevolent guardian spirits. After all, they determined what sort of harvest there'd been and what sort there'd be in the coming year.

One farm housed a sauna elf named Manu. Christmas was a pleasant season for him because he happened to be an elf who enjoyed good food. All through the year the livestock heard Manu muttering to himself as he made his nightly rounds of the cattle barn: "If only it were Christmas, I could eat all night long." At Christmas, you see, all the Christmas dishes were left out on the table overnight so the elf could help himself to the delicacies.

Christmas rolled around once more. That morning the folks woke up earlier than usual because they wanted to complete their chores as quickly as possible

so as to get on with the Yuletide festivities. The horses were fed and the cows milked. Fresh straw was spread in the barn and stable. The mistress was seeing to the preparation of the last of the Christmas dishes. The master of the household brought in fresh, fragrant straw and spread it on the floor. That made it a good place for the children to romp. The house was decorated with ornaments of straw, and Grandfather had whittled a lovely cross for the table. The sauna was being heated early so everyone could finish bathing before dusk. For the birds a beautiful golden sheaf of grain was placed in the yard and seeds were scattered on the ramp to the barn.

Manu the sauna elf watched the folks bustle about and waited impatiently for them to go out to the sauna. You see, it had been the custom since the olden days to set the table with the Christmas meal before going to the sauna so that the guardian spirit could have first go at the goodies.

Everyone soon left for the sauna. The elf dashed eagerly into the house. The fragrance of fresh straw and baking nearly bowled him over. This was the aroma of Christmas. And, oh, how beautiful the house was! All those straw ornaments and crosses and home-made candles, and that wonderful Christmas table! That's what interested Manu most. The table, covered with a white cloth, was spread with a splendid feast....

He found white and dark bread, butter, huge cheeses, milk, smoked meat, porridge, sweet coffee bread, beer, and delectable smelling rutabaga casseroles. There was even some rock candy that the master had brought from town. Manu, eyes popping

and mouth watering, beheld the sumptuous repast. He hardly knew where to begin. He circled the table slowly, nibbling at the meat, dark bread and rutabaga casserole – and even gobbling up a sweet lump of rock candy.

Meanwhile, the folks had finished bathing, and Manu heard them returning to the house. The elf nipped out quick as a wink. People always left the sauna rather hastily because they believed that any slowpoke the elf caught loafing in the steam would be thrown out in the cold snow. Manu found such haste amusing. As far as he was concerned, they could stay in the sauna as long as they liked; that way he'd have more time to sample the Christmas treats. Whatever puts such silly notions into people's heads?

As the folks came in from the yard, Manu crept silently to the sauna, where a fresh head of steam awaited him. He climbed straight up to the warm sauna loft. In no time at all the old greybeard was sound asleep in the darkness. Christmas made it worth being an elf.

At the house everyone was enjoying the bountiful Christmas meal. Back then people believed that if there wasn't food enough to last through the holiday, it meant poverty would come to the household. So plenty of food was laid on.

After the meal the children frolicked in the fresh straw and the family played all sorts of Yuletide games, until sleep brought the festivities to an end.

Around midnight Manu woke up in the sauna loft. From a hiding place under the sauna, he brought out some candles he'd hidden there during the year. He

trudged first to the barn and then to the stable to share some Christmas cheer with the horses, cows and sheep. He lit the candles, chatted a while with the animals and wished them a merry Christmas. Then, in a festive mood, he returned to the house, made certain the folks were really asleep, and went inside. For Manu this was the high point of the Christmas season. There it was on the table, all that food, and a plump candle left burning for the elf. The old guardian spirit crept softly to the table, helped himself to a big bowl of porridge, spooned on a fine pat of butter and, with solemn devotion, commenced to gorge himself.

Manu had seen more Christmases than he could count, but they all had this same warmth in common. There the old elf sat in the Yuletide twilight, the bowl of porridge before him. It was Christmas, when you could eat all night long.

Original Finnish edition *Suomalainen tonttukirja*

published by Otava Publishing Company Ltd 1979

© 1979 Mauri and Tarja Kunnas

English translation © Tim Steffa

1999

All rights reserved.

Printed in Finland by Otava

Publishing Company Ltd 1999

ISBN 951-1-16280-2

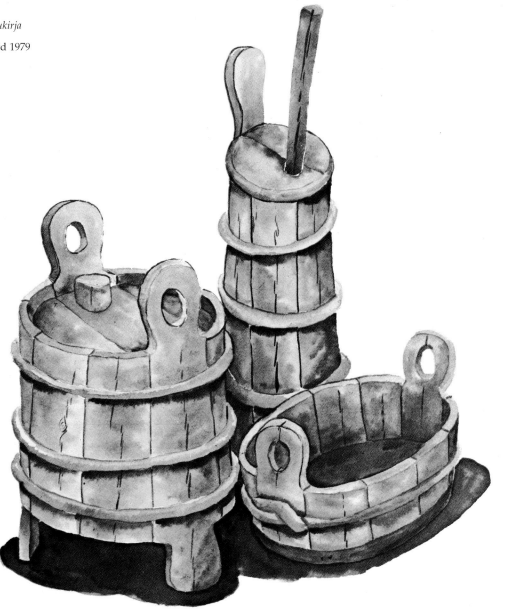